Brilliant Battle Strategies

Children's Military & War History Books

BABY PROFESSOR

EDUCATION KIDS

Speedy Publishing LLC
40 E. Main St. #1156
Newark, DE 19711
www.speedypublishing.com
Copyright 2016

If your army has more soldiers than your enemy's army, it does not automatically mean that you will win the war.

There are many instances in the history of warfare that a smaller force has gained victory through tactics.

There are many war
strategies that have
been developed.
Let's look at some
that have proved
to be effective.

SURPRISE
ATTACK

In 9 AD, the Roman governor, Varus, was lured into an ambush planned by Arminius, who was a Romanized German officer of an auxiliary cavalry unit. Varus went with his three legions through the Teutoborg Forest to suppress the Germanic Revolt.

However, when his 20,000 men were strung out along the line of march, they were surprised by the army of Armenius.

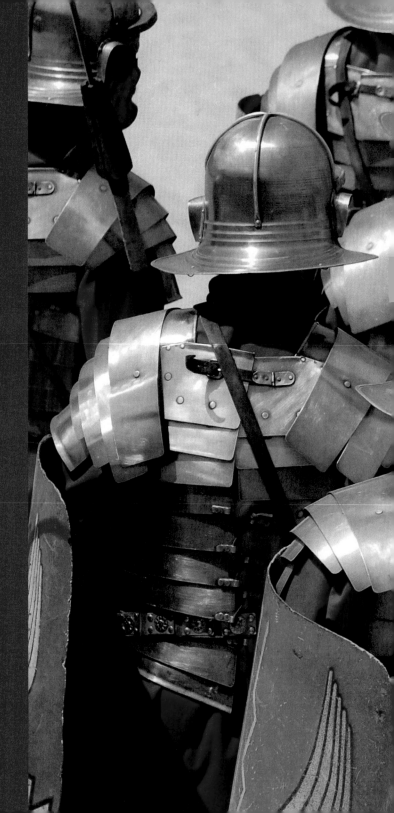

It took several days of struggle until the surviving Romans made a last stand at the Kalkriese Hill, located in the north of present-day Osnabruck. They were wiped out.

Ambushes require careful siting and patience, with precise coordination of each strike arm. The Germanic tribesmen succeeded because of their great discipline in waiting for the exact moment to spring their attack.

ENVELOPMENT

The unexpected appearance of enemy troops from behind or on a flank can damage an army's morale, and if they are encircled, they are deprived of supplies and can be attacked on any side. When they are completely cut off, they must either surrender or fight to the death.

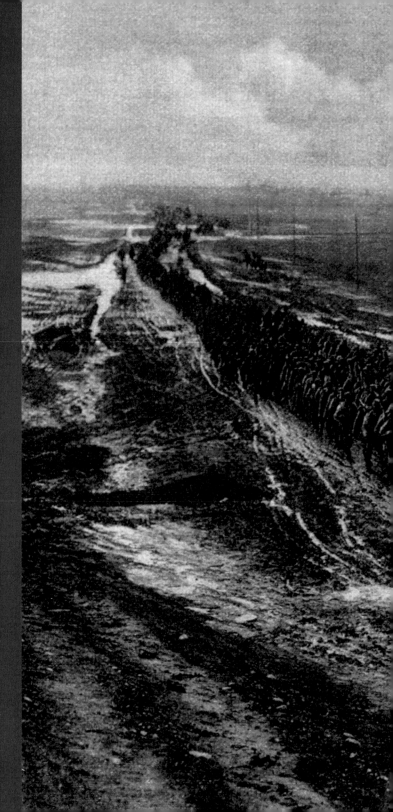

This strategy was employed at the Russian city of Stalingrad in Operation Uranus in November, 1942. The invading Germans were pinned down and unable to maneuver when the Soviets delivered a heavy artillery bombardment of 3,500 guns on troop positions on either side of the city.

They then unleashed several armored divisions with three tank corps. They combined speed and mobility with devastating fire power. The German forces were cut off from resources and could not respond.

DECEPTION

In order for this to work, deception has to establish significant doubt in the mind of the enemy so that they alter their plans. In World War I, the Royal Navy struggled to find solution to U-boat attacks in the Atlantic Ocean.

To gain advantage in this battle, they deployed Q-ships, which were civilian vessels with hidden armaments. When the U-boat surfaced to attack, the Q-ships dropped their side panels to clear the line of fire for the hidden guns. Then the Q-ships attacked the U-boats.

STRATEGIC
OFFENSE AND
TACTICAL
DEFENSE

In war, it's advised that the soldiers should advance into a region that has strategic advantage, like a hill, the ford of a river, or some other strong point. Once they reach that place, they have to set up a tactical defense to force the enemy to make a costly attack.

Babur of Kabul used this tactic in India. He only had 12,000 men while his enemy had 100,000. Babur's troops travelled quickly to Panipat near Delhi, knowing that this sudden threat would prevent the enemy from seeking refuge behind Delhi's walls.

Babur carefully selected the battlefield and formed barriers of wagons. After Lodi's men made a series of fruitless assaults, Babur then made a counter-attack and won the battle.

Did you enjoy reading this book? Share this to your friends.

Visit

BABY PROFESSOR
EDUCATION KIDS

www.BabyProfessorBooks.com

to download Free Baby Professor eBooks
and view our catalog of new and exciting
Children's Books

Made in the USA
Middletown, DE
05 March 2018